**Put Beginning Readers on the Right Track with
ALL ABOARD READING**

The All Aboard Reading series is especially for beginning readers. Written by noted authors and illustrated in full color, these are books that children really and truly *want* to read—books to excite their imagination, tickle their funny bone, expand their interests, and support their feelings. With four different reading levels, All Aboard Reading lets you choose which books are most appropriate for your children and their growing abilities.

Picture Readers—for Ages 3 to 6
Picture Readers have super-simple texts with many nouns appearing as rebus pictures. At the end of each book are 24 flash cards—on one side is the rebus picture; on the other side is the written-out word.

Level 1—for Preschool through First Grade Children
Level 1 books have very few lines per page, very large type, easy words, lots of repetition, and pictures with visual "cues" to help children figure out the words on the page.

Level 2—for First Grade to Third Grade Children
Level 2 books are printed in slightly smaller type than Level 1 books. The stories are more complex, but there is still lots of repetition in the text and many pictures. The sentences are quite simple and are broken up into short lines to make reading easier.

Level 3—for Second Grade through Third Grade Children
Level 3 books have considerably longer texts, use harder words and more complicated sentences.

All Aboard for happy reading!

To Molly—S.A.K.

To Megan, Andrea, Paige, and Britany—J.C.

Photo credits: p. 15, J. Barry Mittan; p. 25, Tom Collins Tour; p. 36, Ingrid Butt/International Figure Skating; p. 47 and back cover, Proper Marketing Associates.

Text copyright © 1997 by S. A. Kramer. Illustrations copyright © 1997 by Jim Campbell. All rights reserved. Published by Grosset & Dunlap, Inc., a member of The Putnam & Grosset Group, New York. ALL ABOARD READING is a trademark of The Putnam & Grosset Group. GROSSET & DUNLAP is a trademark of Grosset & Dunlap, Inc. Published simultaneously in Canada. Printed in the U.S.A.

Library of Congress Cataloging-in-Publication Data

Kramer, Sydelle.
    Ice stars / by S. A. Kramer ; illustrated by Jim Campbell.
      p.   cm. — (All aboard reading. Level 3)
    Summary: Presents brief sketches of four top female figure skaters: Kristi Yamaguchi, Nancy Kerrigan, Oksana Baiul, and Michelle Kwan.
    1. Women skaters—Biography—Juvenile literature. [1. Ice skaters. 2. Women—Biography.] I. Campbell, Jim, 1942– ill. II. Title. III. Series.
GV850.A2K73   1997
796.91'092'2—dc21
[B]
                                                                          96-48022
                                                                           CIP
                                                                             AC

ISBN 0-448-41649-2 (GB)   A B C D E F G H I J
ISBN 0-448-41590-9 (pbk)   A B C D E F G H I J

**Level 3
Grades 2-3**

ICE STARS

**By S. A. Kramer
Illustrated by Jim Campbell**

With photographs

Grosset & Dunlap • New York

America's Sweetheart

July 12, 1971. There's a beautiful new baby in the Yamaguchi family—Kristi. But something is terribly wrong. Her feet are twisted and turned in. The doctor says she has clubfeet. Kristi may never walk like other people.

Until she's a year old, Kristi wears plaster casts on her feet. For three years after that, she wears special shoes. At night she must put on a brace. Looking back she says, "It hurt so bad."

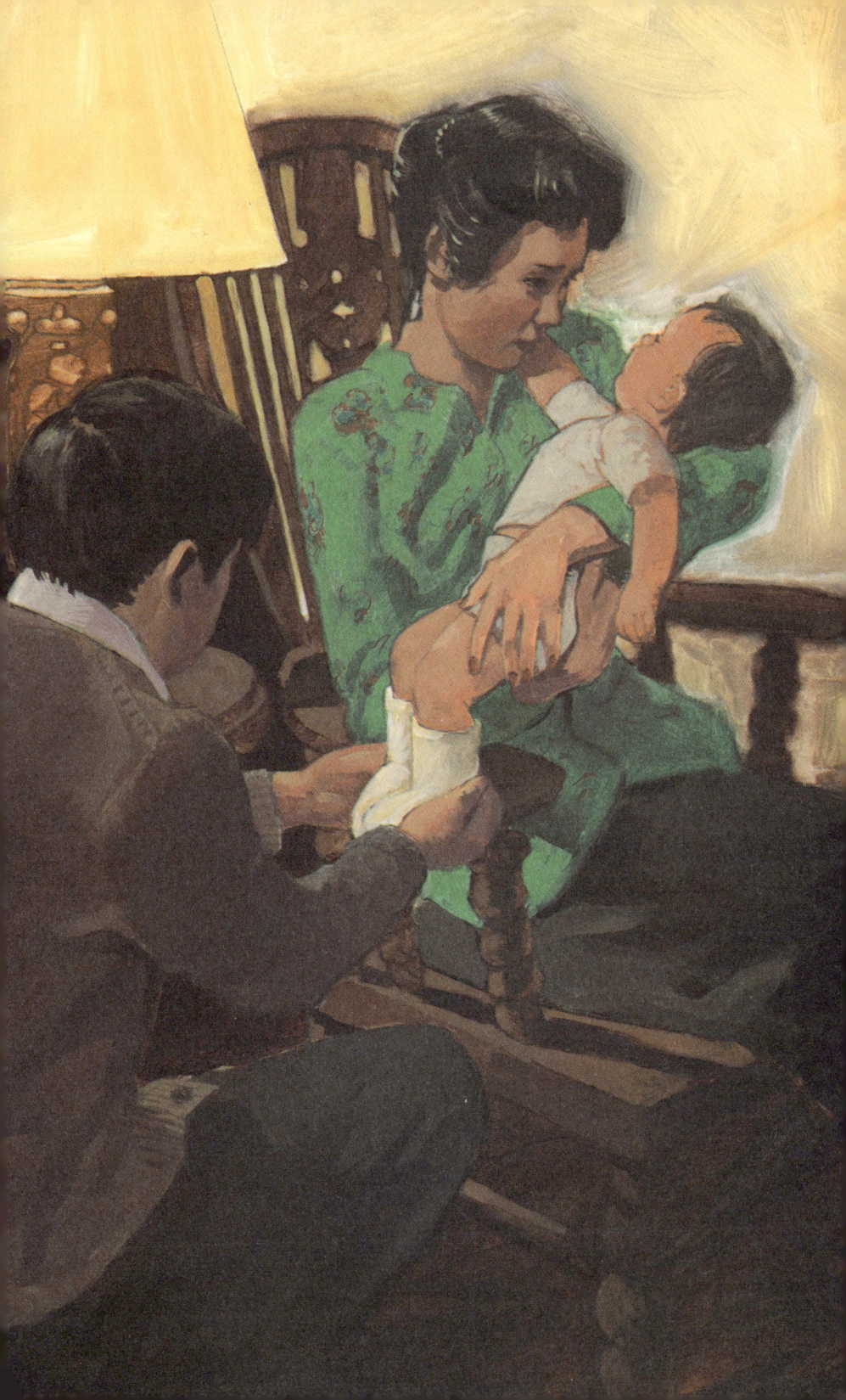

More than anything, Kristi wants to walk like other kids. She ignores the pain and does what the doctors tell her. By the time she's five, her feet are much better. But her legs are weak. She has trouble keeping her balance.

One day Kristi goes to an ice show. She adores the costumes and music. When her older sister goes skating, Kristi begs to skate too. Her mother finally agrees.

But as soon as she steps on the ice, her legs feel shaky. Her mom has to skate with her and hold her up. That doesn't matter to Kristi. She is sure she'll get stronger.

She's right. Skating builds her leg muscles. Soon she's doing jumps. By the time she's eight, she's in contests.

The older Kristi gets, the more she's at the rink. By twelve, she's skating singles <u>and</u> pairs. At sixteen, she's the U.S. junior champion in both events.

She practices all the time. That makes it hard to go to school. For a while she studies at home with a tutor. But Kristi misses her friends too much.

Back to school she goes. That means she has to get up at 3:45 every morning. Then she practices five hours straight. By 10:30 she's in class. At night she crams in her homework—bedtime is 7:30!

By 1989, Kristi has left the juniors behind. That's when she does something no other woman has done since 1954. She wins medals in both singles and pairs at the U.S. championships. In 1990, she does it again.

Now the Olympics are coming up. Kristi knows she must be at her best to make the team. If she skates in just one event, she'll have more time to practice.

Kristi quits pairs. She gets better and better in singles. Smooth and fast, she becomes America's most artistic skater. In 1991, she wins the world championship.

Kristi's moves are hard, but she makes them look easy. She seems to float across the rink. She never gets tired, even after seven triple jumps. Her landings are so soft she could be skating on feathers.

Her size helps her stay light on her feet. Kristi is five feet tall and weighs ninety-three pounds. Her skates are size three. Her dress size is only a one. But Kristi is much stronger than she looks. She can lift 155-pound weights.

In 1992, Kristi wins the U.S. championship. That means she's made it to the Olympics!

On February 21, Kristi skates for gold. The whole world is watching the finals. It's enough to make anyone nervous. But Kristi is calm—she even takes a nap before skating. When she's on the rink, her black-and-gold costume glitters in the lights. She doesn't hear or see anyone else, she's thinking so hard about her program.

She falls once. Will it cost her the gold? No—the judges still believe she's the best. Kristi becomes the first American woman to win the gold medal since 1976! "I've dreamed about this since I was a little girl," she says.

Kristi is the first Japanese-American athlete to become a star. Later in 1992, she wins the world title again. Today she skates in ice shows just like the one that made her fall in love with skating. She still trains up to eight hours a day. But no matter what, she finds time for rollerblading and shopping.

Off the ice, Kristi is quiet, even shy. She has never let her success go to her head. On the rink, she's confident and proud. That's where, she says, "I feel like I can do anything."

The Ice Princess

Detroit, Michigan. January 6, 1994. Practice is over. Nancy Kerrigan is the last to leave the ice. She's been training hard—the U.S. championships are only two days away. Nancy's favored to win and go on to the Olympics. It looks as if she's going to become a star.

Twenty-four years old, Nancy has waited years for this chance. She began skating at the age of six. Back then, she was a tomboy. Now she's grown into an athlete. Her good looks and lovely costumes show off her natural style and grace.

Still in her skates, Nancy walks toward the locker room. She doesn't see a man in a black cap behind her. He's carrying a long metal stick. Suddenly he smashes it into her right knee!

Nancy screams. She falls backward onto the red carpet. Tears are pouring from her eyes. Her father rushes to her side. She looks up at him. "Why me? Why now?" she cries.

Nancy's knee is swollen and sore. The next day she can't even bend it. She limps when she walks. Luckily, nothing is broken. But there's no way she can skate in the championships now. Could her dream of stardom be over?

Nancy's shaken and scared. The attack has come at a very important point in her career. Last year she flopped at the world championships. This year she was coming back.

At the world championships, Nancy fell apart. Behind her big smile and cool look, she was afraid of doing badly. She seemed to forget she was the 1993 U.S. champ, and the bronze medalist at the 1992 Olympics. Nancy got so nervous she couldn't make some of her jumps.

Afterward she made herself a promise. She'd prove to everyone she was good enough to win. Ever since, she's been working hard.

The Olympic team invites Nancy to skate even though she missed the U.S. championships. She has only weeks to get back in shape. Can she recover in time?

She lifts weights...

and swims.

She rides an exercise bike.

To help herself relax, she listens to comedy tapes.

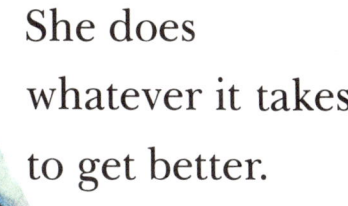

She does whatever it takes to get better.

Then she hears shocking news. Another skater was mixed up in the attack. It's someone Nancy knows—Tonya Harding. If Nancy weren't around, Tonya would be America's best. Was Tonya trying to get her out of the way?

Nancy is angry. But she keeps her feelings to herself. Without a word of complaint, she works to make her leg stronger. She's not going to let anyone rob her of her right to skate.

At the Olympic finals, Nancy's hard work pays off. She takes to the ice as if she had never been hurt. In a beautiful white dress, she looks just like a princess. And she gives her best performance ever.

Yet she doesn't win the gold medal. The judges think Oksana Baiul is more artistic. Oksana beats Nancy by a tenth of a point. Nancy must settle for silver. Many people think the judges are wrong.

Nancy is terribly disappointed. She's come so far—yet she still hasn't won. To her fans, it doesn't seem fair.

Her family agrees. They've always believed in Nancy. For years they struggled to keep her on the ice. Her training cost more than $50,000 a year. It has never been easy for them.

Her father worked three jobs and borrowed money. Her mom helped as much as she could, although she is almost blind. Nancy's two brothers pitched in.

But even though Nancy didn't win the gold, fans everywhere want to see her. Nancy's a star!

Today she's a professional skater. She's married and has a baby. She still wishes she'd won the gold, but it's not so important anymore. Nancy has new dreams now.

The Swan

Oksana Baiul speeds backward on the ice. Just sixteen years old, she's practicing for the Olympic finals tomorrow. It's February 24, 1994, and she's in Lillehammer, Norway. There's only one thing on her mind: Can she win the gold medal?

From the corner of her eye, Oksana spots another skater. The girl doesn't see her—they're on a crash course! The girl slams full speed into Oksana.

They tumble to the ice. Oksana needs help getting up. She's gashed her right leg. Even worse, she's twisted her back.

Oksana needs three stitches in her leg. The pain in her back won't go away. Her doctors tell her she shouldn't skate in the finals.

Oksana won't listen. She tries to practice the next morning. But her legs shake and wobble. She can't bend.

She limps from the rink. Tears soak her face. People watching are sure she won't skate tonight.

They don't know Oksana. This teenager from Ukraine has suffered too much to give up now.

When she was two, her father left home and never came back. Soon the grandparents she loved died. Then came the hardest loss of all. Her mother got sick. By the time Oksana was thirteen, her mother was dead. Oksana was an orphan.

All she had left was her skating. She'd been training since the age of three. But now she didn't even have a coach—he had moved to another country. Oksana was poor and alone. Sometimes she had nowhere to sleep but the rink.

Then her luck changed. She found a new coach and went to live with her. Oksana's friend Viktor Petrenko, an Olympic champion, bought her new costumes and skates. In 1993, she won the world championship—the youngest to do it in seventy years.

With her long legs, Oksana was fast on the ice. Her jumps were high. She seemed lighter than air. Fans called her "the swan" because she was so graceful. It was hard to believe she was once too chubby to be a ballerina.

Now Oksana has made it to the Olympics. But will she be able to skate? It seems impossible that she can win a medal with her injuries.

An hour before she performs, doctors give her two shots of painkillers. She tells herself to forget how sore she is. To honor her mother, she must win the gold medal.

Oksana enters the rink. Her hands are shaking. She thinks of her mother and feels stronger. The music starts. It seems to fill her body. As she skates, people can't take their eyes off her.

Her glowing smile makes them feel good. Her wide green eyes leave them feeling sad. All of her movements are full of emotion. One judge thinks she's skating "from the heart, the inside."

But she fouls a jump. There's just a minute left in her program. To win, she has to make up for her mistake.

All at once she whips off a triple-toe loop, then a double-axel, double-toe combination. Her program is over. What a way to finish!

Oksana knows she did well. But was it

enough for a medal? Her scores flash on the board—they are almost all 5.8's and 5.9's.

She wins the gold medal! She cries and laughs at the same time. Oksana is the youngest Olympic champion since 1928. She says, "My mother was with me at the moment of victory."

Success gives Oksana a new life. She moves to Connecticut and stars in ice shows all over the country. She even looks different, with her new hairdo and stylish clothes. Fans can tell she's growing up fast.

Yet Oksana's past is always with her. To this day, she wears a ring that belonged to her grandmother. At times sadness darkens her eyes. But skating, she says, ". . . helps me get over the pain. Skating is my life."

Picture Perfect

"What am I going to do?" Michelle Kwan asks herself. It's March 23, 1996. China's Chen Lu has just taken the lead in the world championships. There's only one way Michelle can win now. She has to skate perfectly. Can she do it?

If anyone can, it's Michelle. She's only fifteen, but she's a terrific athlete. She hardly ever falls. Her jumps are clean and powerful. This year, she won the U.S. championships. But is she enough of an artist to be judged the world's best?

Just last year, Michelle looked and acted like a kid. Her skills were sharp, but her style was stiff. The judges didn't award her any medals. Michelle seemed too young to be a champion.

But she's changed a lot in a year. She used to have a ponytail—today her hair is pulled up into a bun. Last year she didn't wear makeup—now she puts it on every time she performs. Tonight she even has little jewels at the corners of her eyes.

Her music is more grown-up too. When she skates, she acts the role of a woman, not a girl. Even her costume is older—a harem skirt and a halter top, made of dazzling purple beads. Michelle hardly looks like the person the world saw last year.

As she steps onto the ice, the crowd claps and cheers. But Michelle seems nervous. Outside, the temperature is below zero. Inside, Michelle feels only heat. She tells herself, "Just go for it."

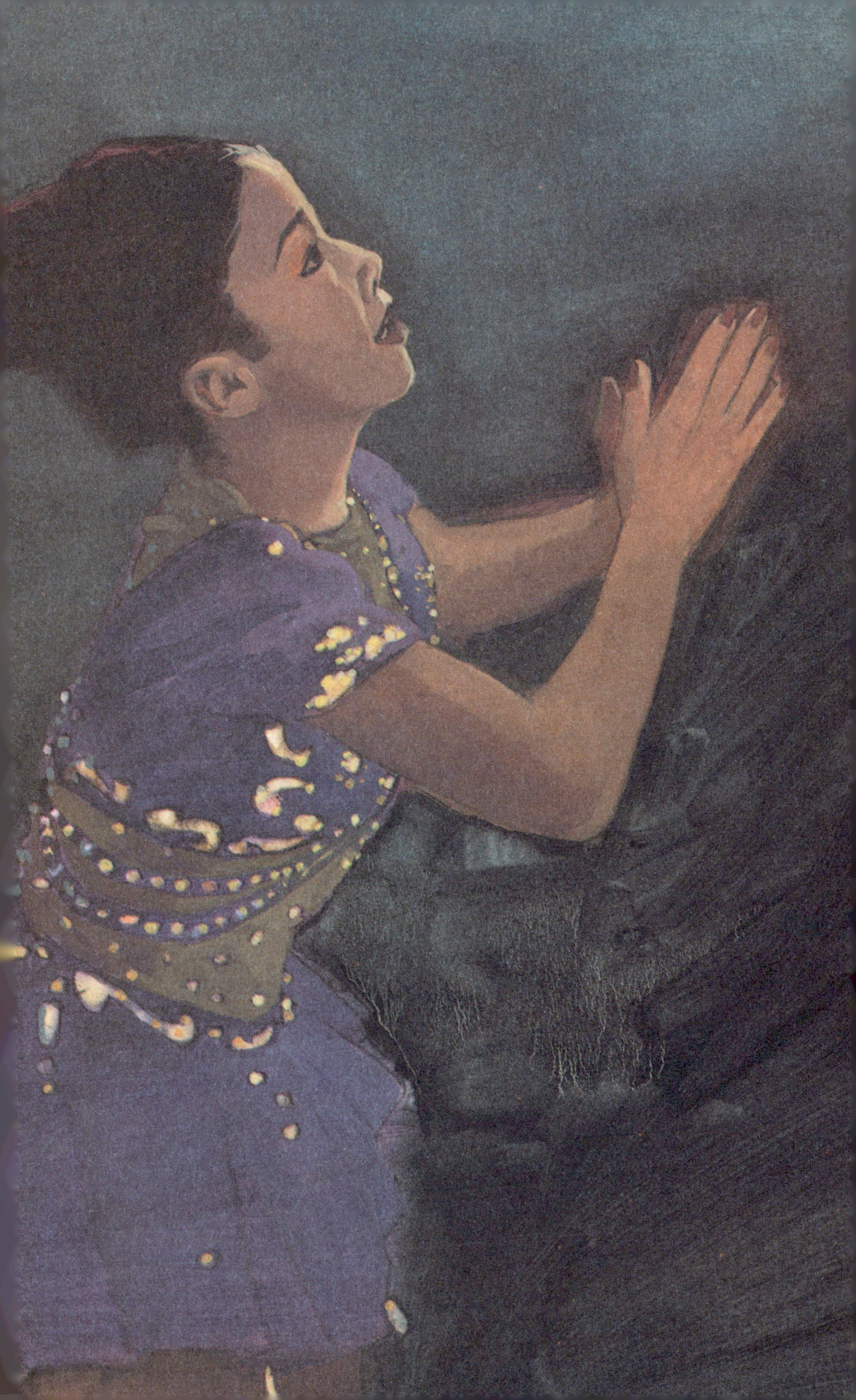

Then the music starts. Can she make her first jump? It's a triple-lutz, double-toe combination. Yes! Now she's calm and in control. She imagines she's the wind, "flying everywhere." Her graceful hands reach out toward the crowd.

Michelle wants to win, badly. But suddenly she's in trouble. She has to cut a triple-toe loop down to a double. It's not a huge mistake, but it's enough to give Chen Lu the lead. Now Michelle has only one chance. She must do something special.

At the end of her program, she throws in a triple-toe jump. If she makes it, she knows she'll finish first. If she doesn't, she'll lose.

Michelle hits it perfectly! It's the seventh triple jump of her program. The judges know that's the mark of a champion.

The crowd leaps up and cheers. Michelle sobs, then smiles. Her hands cover her face. She's won! "I'm just very happy," she says later. "I can't believe it."

Michelle has become the third-youngest world champion ever. In just one year, she's gone from a girl of promise to America's best hope for Olympic gold.

Michelle started to skate at age five. At first she could barely keep her balance. But she stuck with it. Her brother played hockey, and she wanted to be like him.

Then, when she was seven, Michelle watched the 1988 Olympics. She couldn't take her eyes off the skaters twirling through the air. That's when she knew she wanted to do what they did.

Her parents cheered her on. They paid for private lessons. Right away, Michelle's talent was clear. In only a few months, she was winning contests.

She practiced so much that by eighth grade she stopped going to school. Instead, she has a private tutor. She's lonely at times; she says she has no social life.

Like every top skater, five-foot-two inch Michelle must watch her weight. She weighs a hundred pounds—and anything extra can throw her jumps off. That's why she eats chocolate only once a week.

Michelle knows what she wants. But tough as she is, she can get nervous when she has to compete. Sometimes she worries so much she talks in her sleep.

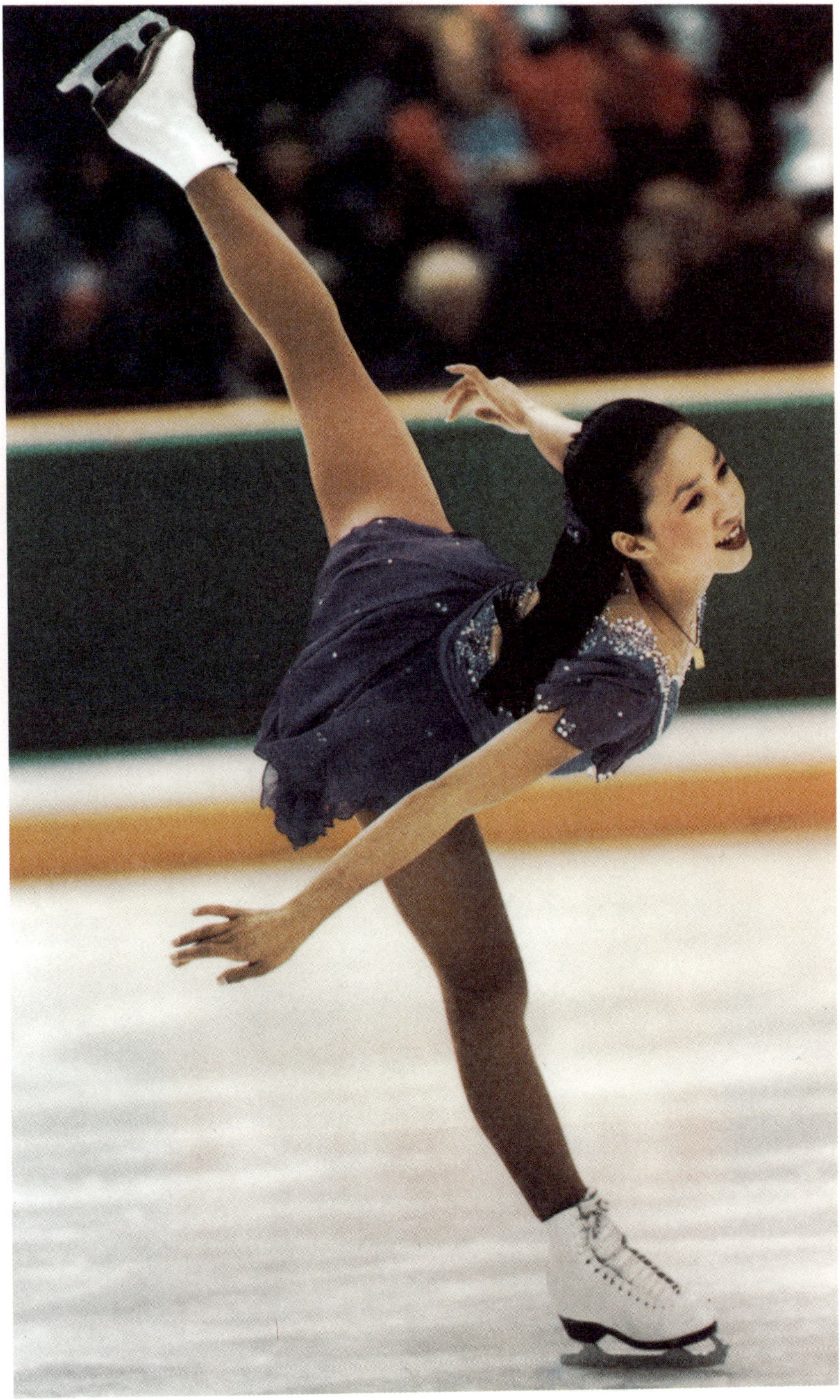

When she's feeling bad, Michelle turns to her family. They are Chinese-American, and very close. Her older sister Karen, also a skater, is her best friend.

Michelle is one of America's brightest skating stars. She's proved she's a real artist. But she hopes for even more. She says, "I want to be a legend."

	DATE DUE		

20248

920   Kramer, Sydelle.
KRA
            Ice stars

WAYNE ELEM. SCHOOL LIBRARY
WAYNE, PA. 19087

755085 00988   33702C   005